BRIGGFLATTS

Basil Bunting on his last visit to Brigflatts meeting house in 1984. (Photo: Derek Smith)

BASIL BUNTING

BRIGGFLATTS

WITH CD OF *BRIGGFLATTS* READ BY BASIL BUNTING

& DVD OF PETER BELL'S FILM OF BASIL BUNTING

BLOODAXE BOOKS

ISBN: 978 1 85224 826 0

This edition published 2009 by
Bloodaxe Books Ltd,
Eastburn,
South Park,
Hexham
Northumberland NE46 1BS.

Reprinted 2009, 2010, 2011, 2018, 2022

www.bloodaxebooks.com
For further information about Bloodaxe titles
please visit our website or write to
the above address for a catalogue.

Supported using public funding by
ARTS COUNCIL
ENGLAND

Cover design: Neil Astley & Pamela Robertson-Pearce.

CD and DVD manufactured by Sound Performance.

Printed in Great Britain by
Bell & Bain Limited, Glasgow, Scotland.

CONTENTS

Basil Bunting at Greystead Cottage, Tarset, in 1982. (Photo: Derek Smith)

Readings and texts of *Briggflatts*

Basil Bunting gave the first public reading of *Briggflatts* at Morden Tower, Newcastle, on 22 December 1965. It was first published in the January 1966 issue of the American magazine *Poetry*, and first published in book form in February 1966 in a large format limited edition by Fulcrum Press (with a few errors corrected from its first publication in *Poetry*). A trade edition paperback followed from Fulcrum in December 1966, and there were subsequent reprints from Fulcrum of this separate edition of *Briggflatts* in hardback and paperback.

Briggflatts was reprinted in all the collected editions of Bunting's work: *Collected Poems* (Fulcrum Press, 1968 & 1970); *Collected Poems* (Oxford University Press, 1978); *The Complete Poems* (Oxford University Press, 1994); and *Complete Poems* (Bloodaxe Books, 2000), accompanied by the double-cassette *Basil Bunting reads 'Briggflatts' and other poems* (Bloodaxe Books, 2000). The text of *Briggflatts* used in this edition (including the author's notes) is identical to that of *Complete Poems* (2000), which remains in print in that edition from Bloodaxe Books as well as in the American edition of the same book published by New Directions in 2003. Bunting's notes on the poem were titled 'Afterthoughts' in the original Fulcrum edition of *Briggflatts*; in subsequent collected editions they appeared under the collective heading of 'Notes'.

'A Note on *Briggflatts*', which follows Bunting's text and notes in this edition, originated from a typescript whose history is explained by Richard Caddel in the footnote. It was first published as a separate pamphlet by the Basil Bunting Poetry Archive at Durham University Library in 1989, and has not previously been published in editions of Bunting's work.

The first studio recording of *Briggflatts* was made in 1967 at the home of Stuart and Deirdre Montgomery in Southampton Row, London, by John Cassidy and produced for Stream Records (1968) by Fred Hunter. Reissued on cassette by Keele University in 1988, it was later included in *The Recordings of Basil Bunting*, edited by Richard Swigg, a set of 8 cassettes issued by Keele University in association with the Basil Bunting Poetry Centre at Durham University in 1994. It is this recording which was used on the double-cassette issued by Bloodaxe Books in 2000, and which is now released again, for the first time on CD, with this edition of *Briggflatts*. Many thanks are due to Fred Hunter and John Cassidy for their permission to re-release their recording, and to Dave Maughan at Face Musical Productions for his expert sound editing and digital mastering.

Two of the poem's structural models were the interlaced ornamentation of the Lindisfarne Gospels (see front cover of this book), and the Scarlatti sonata. Bunting also gave some readings of *Briggflatts* with the accompaniment of Domenico Scarlatti sonatas on harpsichord, including one video-recorded at Aidanvision Studios in Carlisle in 1977, whose soundtrack was released by Bloodaxe Books in 1980 as an LP record, *Basil Bunting reads 'Briggflatts'*. Scarlatti's sonata in B minor, L.33, was an important catalyst in the conception of *Briggflatts*, and that recording shows how closely that sonata is echoed in the poem in the second part of the fourth movement, where it accompanies the reading; it is repeated after the coda. Bunting's full reading of *Briggflatts* with Scarlatti's music included other sonatas played between the movements. The first such reading to be recorded on tape was one he gave in Canada at the University of British Columbia in 1970.

Peter Bell's film *Basil Bunting: An introduction to the work of a poet* was made by Northeast Films and first shown on Channel Four in 1982. Most of the film was shot around Brigflatts meeting house near Sedbergh, Cumbria, and at Greystead Cottage in Northumberland's Tarset valley, where Bunting lived from 1981 to 1984. This film and all films in the Arts Council England film collection can be streamed to users in universities and colleges in the UK (with an ac.uk suffix) from the Arts On Film website, which is owned and managed by the University of Westminster. The Arts Council England film collection contains almost 500 titles dating back to the 1950s and is housed with Arts Council England. Special thanks are due to Arts Council England for permission to include the film on DVD with this edition, and to Gill Johnson, Richard Gooderick and Peter Bell.

The film has been converted for the DVD to the PAL format used in Britain and Europe. It cannot be played on American DVD players which require DVDs to be NTSC format, but it should be playable on most computers with DVD software.

Thanks are due to the Estate of Basil Bunting and to the Basil Bunting Poetry Archive at Durham University (the source of most of the photographs) for their help and continuing cooperation, and to Don Share for permission to use extracts from his 'Short notes on a longish poem', the longer version of which can be found at donshare.blogspot.com/2008/05/short-notes-on-longish-poem.html

BRIGGFLATTS

An Autobiography

For Peggy

Son los pasariellos del mal pelo exidos

The spuggies are fledged

I

Brag, sweet tenor bull,
descant on Rawthey's madrigal,
each pebble its part
for the fells' late spring.
Dance tiptoe, bull,
black against may.
Ridiculous and lovely
chase hurdling shadows
morning into noon.
May on the bull's hide
and through the dale
furrows fill with may,
paving the slowworm's way.

A mason times his mallet
to a lark's twitter,
listening while the marble rests,
lays his rule
at a letter's edge,
fingertips checking,
till the stone spells a name
naming none,
a man abolished.
Painful lark, labouring to rise!
The solemn mallet says:
In the grave's slot
he lies. We rot.

Decay thrusts the blade,
wheat stands in excrement
trembling. Rawthey trembles.
Tongue stumbles, ears err
for fear of spring.
Rub the stone with sand,
wet sandstone rending
roughness away. Fingers
ache on the rubbing stone.
The mason says: Rocks
happen by chance.
No one here bolts the door,
love is so sore.

Stone smooth as skin,
cold as the dead they load
on a low lorry by night.
The moon sits on the fell
but it will rain.
Under sacks on the stone
two children lie,
hear the horse stale,
the mason whistle,
harness mutter to shaft,
felloe to axle squeak,
rut thud the rim,
crushed grit.

Stocking to stocking, jersey to jersey,
head to a hard arm,
they kiss under the rain,
bruised by their marble bed.
In Garsdale, dawn;
at Hawes, tea from the can.
Rain stops, sacks
steam in the sun, they sit up.
Copper-wire moustache,
sea-reflecting eyes
and Baltic plainsong speech
declare: By such rocks
men killed Bloodaxe.

Fierce blood throbs in his tongue,
lean words.
Skulls cropped for steel caps
huddle round Stainmore.
Their becks ring on limestone,
whisper to peat.
The clogged cart pushes the horse downhill.
In such soft air
they trudge and sing,
laying the tune frankly on the air.
All sounds fall still,
fellside bleat,
hide-and-seek peewit.

Her pulse their pace,
palm countering palm,
till a trench is filled,
stone white as cheese
jeers at the dale.
Knotty wood, hard to rive,
smoulders to ash;
smell of October apples.
The road again,
at a trot.
Wetter, warmed, they watch
the mason meditate
on name and date.

Rain rinses the road,
the bull streams and laments.
Sour rye porridge from the hob
with cream and black tea,
meat, crust and crumb.
Her parents in bed
the children dry their clothes.
He has untied the tape
of her striped flannel drawers
before the range. Naked
on the pricked rag mat
his fingers comb
thatch of his manhood's home.

Gentle generous voices weave
over bare night
words to confirm and delight
till bird dawn.
Rainwater from the butt
she fetches and flannel
to wash him inch by inch,
kissing the pebbles.
Shining slowworm part of the marvel.
The mason stirs:
Words!
Pens are too light.
Take a chisel to write.

Every birth a crime,
every sentence life.
Wiped of mould and mites
would the ball run true?
No hope of going back.
Hounds falter and stray,
shame deflects the pen.
Love murdered neither bleeds nor stifles
but jogs the draftsman's elbow.
What can he, changed, tell
her, changed, perhaps dead?
Delight dwindles. Blame
stays the same.

Brief words are hard to find,
shapes to carve and discard:
Bloodaxe, king of York,
king of Dublin, king of Orkney.
Take no notice of tears;
letter the stone to stand
over love laid aside lest
insufferable happiness impede
flight to Stainmore,
to trace
lark, mallet,
becks, flocks
and axe knocks.

Dung will not soil the slowworm's
mosaic. Breathless lark
drops to nest in sodden trash;
Rawthey truculent, dingy.
Drudge at the mallet, the may is down,
fog on fells. Guilty of spring
and spring's ending
amputated years ache after
the bull is beef, love a convenience.
It is easier to die than to remember.
Name and date
split in soft slate
a few months obliterate.

II

Poet appointed dare not decline
to walk among the bogus, nothing to authenticate
the mission imposed, despised
by toadies, confidence men, kept boys,
shopped and jailed, cleaned out by whores,
touching acquaintance for food and tobacco.
Secret, solitary, a spy, he gauges
lines of a Flemish horse
hauling beer, the angle, obtuse,
a slut's blouse draws on her chest,
counts beat against beat, bus conductor
against engine against wheels against
the pedal, Tottenham Court Road, decodes
thunder, scans
porridge bubbling, pipes clanking, feels
Buddha's basalt cheek
but cannot name the ratio of its curves
to the half-pint
left breast of a girl who bared it in Kleinfeldt's.
He lies with one to long for another,
sick, self-maimed, self-hating,
obstinate, mating
beauty with squalor to beget lines still-born.

You who can calculate the course
of a biased bowl,
shall I come near the jack?
What twist can counter the force
that holds back
woods I roll?

You who elucidate the disk
hubbed by the sun,
shall I see autumn out
or the fifty years at risk
be lost, doubt
end what's begun?

Under his right oxter the loom of his sweep
the pilot turns from the wake.

Thole-pins shred where the oar leans,
grommets renewed, tallowed;
halliards frapped to the shrouds.
Crew grunt and gasp. Nothing he sees
they see, but hate and serve. Unscarred ocean,
day's swerve, swell's poise, pursuit,
he blends, balances, drawing leagues under the keel
to raise cold cliffs where tides
knot fringes of weed.
No tilled acre, gold scarce,
walrus tusk, whalebone, white bear's liver.
Scurvy gnaws, steading smell, hearth's crackle.
Crabs, shingle, seracs on the icefall.
Summer is bergs and fogs, lichen on rocks.
Who cares to remember a name cut in ice
or be remembered?
Wind writes in foam on the sea:

Who sang, sea takes,
brawn brine, bone grit.
Keener the kittiwake.
Fells forget him.
Fathoms dull the dale,
gulfweed voices . . .

About ship! Sweat in the south. Go bare
because the soil is adorned,
sunset the colour of a boiled louse.
Steep sluice or level,
parts of the sewer ferment faster.
Days jerk, dawdle, fidget
towards the cesspit.
Love is a vapour, we're soon through it.

Flying fish follow the boat,
delicate wings blue, grace
on flick of a tissue tail,
the water's surface between
appetite and attainment.
Flexible, unrepetitive line
to sing, not paint; sing, sing,
laying the tune on the air,

nimble and easy as a lizard,
still and sudden as a gecko,
to humiliate love, remember
nothing.

It tastes good, garlic and salt in it,
with the half-sweet white wine of Orvieto
on scanty grass under great trees
where the ramparts cuddle Lucca.

It sounds right, spoken on the ridge
between marine olives and hillside
blue figs, under the breeze fresh
with pollen of Apennine sage.

It feels soft, weed thick in the cave
and the smooth wet riddance of Antonietta's
bathing suit, mouth ajar for
submarine Amalfitan kisses.

It looks well on the page, but never
well enough. Something is lost
when wind, sun, sea upbraid
justly an unconvinced deserter.

White marble stained like a urinal
cleft in Apuan Alps,
always trickling, apt to the saw. Ice and wedge
split it or well-measured cordite shots,
while paraffin pistons rap, saws rip
and clamour is clad in stillness:
clouds echo marble middens, sugar-white,
that cumber the road stones travel
to list the names of the dead.
There is a lot of Italy in churchyards,
sea on the left, the Garfagnana
over the wall, la Cisa flaking
to hillside fiddlers above Parma,
melancholy, swift,
with light bow blanching the dance.
Grease mingles with sweat
on the threshing floor. Frogs, grasshoppers

drape the rice in sound.
Tortoise deep in dust or
muzzled bear capering
punctuate a text whose initial,
lost in Lindisfarne plaited lines,
stands for discarded love.

Win from rock
    flame and ore.
Crucibles pour
    sanded ingots.

Heat and hammer
    draw out a bar.
Wheel and water
    grind an edge.

No worn tool
    whittles stone;
but a reproached
    uneasy mason

shaping evasive
    ornament
litters his yard
    with flawed fragments.

Loaded with mail of linked lies,
what weapon can the king lift to fight
when chance-met enemies employ sly
sword and shoulder-piercing pike,
pressed into the mire,
trampled and hewn till a knife
– in whose hand? – severs tight
neck cords? Axe rusts. Spine
picked bare by ravens, agile
maggots devour the slack side
and inert brain, never wise.
What witnesses he had life,
ravelled and worn past splice,
yarns falling to staple? Rime
on the bent, the beck ice,

there will be nothing on Stainmore to hide
void, no sable to disguise
what he wore under the lies,
king of Orkney, king of Dublin, twice
king of York, where the tide
stopped till long flight
from who knows what smile,
scowl, disgust or delight
ended in bale on the fellside.

Starfish, poinsettia on a half-tide crag,
a galliard by Byrd.
Anemones spite cullers of ornament
but design the pool
to their grouping. The hermit crab
is no grotesque in such company.

Asian vultures riding on a spiral
column of dust
or swift desert ass startled by the
camels' dogged saunter
figures sudden flight of the descant
on a madrigal by Monteverdi.

But who will entune a bogged orchard,
its blossom gone,
fruit unformed, where hunger and
damp hush the hive?
A disappointed July full of codling
moth and ragged lettuces?

Yet roe are there, rise to the fence, insolent;
a scared vixen cringes
red against privet stems as a mazurka;
and rat, grey, rummaging
behind the compost heap has daring
to thread, lithe and alert, Schoenberg's maze.

Riding silk, adrift on noon,
a spider gleams like a berry
less black than cannibal slug
but no less pat under elders

where shadows themselves are a web.
So is summer held to its contract
and the year solvent; but men
driven by storm fret,
reminded of sweltering Crete
and Pasiphae's pungent sweat,
who heard the god-bull's feet
scattering sand,
breathed byre stink, yet stood
with expectant hand
to guide his seed to its soil;
nor did flesh flinch
distended by the brute
nor loaded spirit sink
till it had gloried in unlike creation.

III

Down into dust and reeds
at the patrolled bounds
where captives thicken to gaze
slither companions, wary, armed,
whose torches straggle
seeking charred hearths
to define a road.
Day, dim, laps at the shore
in petulant ripples
soon smoothed in night
on pebbles worn by tabulation till
only the shell of figures is left
as fragile honeycomb breeze.
Tides of day strew the shingle
tides of night sweep, snoring;
and some turned back, taught
by dreams the year would capsize
where the bank quivers, paved
with gulls stunned on a cliff
not hard to climb, muffled
in flutter, scored by beaks,
pestered by scavengers
whose palms scoop droppings to mould
cakes for hungry towns. One
plucked fruit warm from the arse
of his companion, who
making to beat him, he screamed:
Hastor! Hastor! but Hastor
raised dung thickened lashes to stare
disdaining those who cry:
Sweet shit! Buy!
for he swears in the market:
By God with whom I lunched!
there is no trash in the wheat
my loaf is kneaded from.
Nor will unprofitable motion
stir the stink that settles round him.
Leave given
we would have slaughtered the turd-bakers
but neither whip nor knife

can welt their hide.
Guides at the top claim fees
though the way is random
past hovels hags lean from
rolling lizard eyes
at boys gnawed by the wolf,
past bevelled downs, grey marshes
where some souse in brine
long rotted corpses, others,
needier, sneak through saltings
to snatch toe, forearm, ear,
and on gladly to hills
briar and bramble vest
where beggars advertise
rash, chancre, fistula,
to hug glib shoulders, mingle herpetic
limbs with stumps and cosset the mad.
Some the Laughing Stone disables
whom giggle and snicker waste
till fun suffocates them. Beyond
we heard the teeming falls of the dead,
saw kelts fall back long-jawed, without flesh,
cruel by appetite beyond its term,
straining to bright gravel spawning pools.
Eddies batter them, borne down to the sea,
archipelago of galaxies,
zero suspending the world.
Banners purple and green flash from its walls,
pennants of red, orange blotched pale on blue,
glimmer of ancient arms
to pen and protect mankind.
But we desired Macedonia,
the rocky meadows, horses, barley pancakes,
incest and familiar games,
to end in our place by our own wars,
and deemed the peak unscaleable; but he
reached to a crack in the rock
with some scorn, resolute though in doubt,
traversed limestone to gabbro,
file sharp, skinning his fingers,
and granite numb with ice, in air
too thin to bear up a gnat,

scrutinising holds while day lasted,
groping for holds in the dark
till the morning star reflected
in the glazed crag
and other light not of the sun
dawning from above
lit feathers sweeping snow
and the limbs of Israfel,
trumpet in hand, intent on the east,
cheeks swollen to blow,
whose sigh is cirrus: Yet delay!
When will the signal come
to summon man to his clay?

Heart slow, nerves numb and memory, he lay
on glistening moss by a spring;
as a woodman dazed by an adder's sting
barely within recall
tests the rebate tossed to him, so he
ascertained moss and bracken,
a cold squirm snaking his flank
and breath leaked to his ear:
I am neither snake nor lizard,
I am the slowworm.

Ripe wheat is my lodging. I polish
my side on pillars of its transept,
gleam in its occasional light.
Its swaying
copies my gait.

Vaults stored with slugs to relish,
my quilt a litter of husks, I prosper
lying low, little concerned.
My eyes sharpen
when I blink.

Good luck to reaper and miller!
Grubs adhere even to stubble.
Come plowtime
the ditch is near.

Sycamore seed twirling,
O, writhe to its measure!
Dust swirling trims pleasure.
Thorns prance in a gale.
In air snow flickers,
twigs tap,
elms drip.

Swaggering, shimmering fall,
drench and towel us all!

So he rose and led home silently through clean woodland
where every bough repeated the slowworm's song.

IV

Grass caught in willow tells the flood's height that has subsided;
overfalls sketch a ledge to be bared tomorrow.
No angler homes with empty creel though mist dims day.
I hear Aneurin number the dead, his nipped voice.
Slight moon limps after the sun. A closing door
stirs smoke's flow above the grate. Jangle
to skald, battle, journey; to priest Latin is bland.
Rats have left no potatoes fit to roast, the gamey tang
recalls ibex guts steaming under a cold ridge,
tomcat stink of a leopard dying while I stood
easing the bolt to dwell on a round's shining rim.
I hear Aneurin number the dead and rejoice,
being adult male of a merciless species.
Today's posts are piles to drive into the quaggy past
on which impermanent palaces balance.
I see Aneurin's pectoral muscle swell under his shirt,
pacing between the game Ida left to rat and raven,
young men, tall yesterday, with cabled thighs.
Red deer move less warily since their bows dropped.
Girls in Teesdale and Wensleydale wake discontent.
Clear Cymric voices carry well this autumn night,
Aneurin and Taliesin, cruel owls
for whom it is never altogether dark, crying
before the rules made poetry a pedant's game.
Columba, Columbanus, as the soil shifts its vest,
Aidan and Cuthbert put on daylight,
wires of sharp western metal entangled in its soft
web, many shuttles as midges darting;
not for bodily welfare nor pauper theorems
but splendour to splendour, excepting nothing that is.
Let the fox have his fill, patient leech and weevil,
cattle refer the rising of Sirius to their hedge horizon,
runts murder the sacred calves of the sea by rule
heedless of herring gull, surf and the text carved by waves
on the skerry. Can you trace shuttles thrown
like drops from a fountain, spray, mist of spiderlines
bearing the rainbow, quoits round the draped moon;
shuttles like random dust desert whirlwinds hoy at their tormenting sun?
Follow the clue patiently and you will understand nothing.

Lice in its seams despise the jacket shrunk to the world's core,
crawl with toil to glimpse
from its shoulder walls of flame which could they reach
they'd crackle like popcorn in a skillet.

As the player's breath warms the fipple the tone clears.
It is time to consider how Domenico Scarlatti
condensed so much music into so few bars
with never a crabbed turn or congested cadence,
never a boast or a see-here; and stars and lakes
echo him and the copse drums out his measure,
snow peaks are lifted up in moonlight and twilight
and the sun rises on an acknowledged land.

My love is young but wise. Oak, applewood,
her fire is banked with ashes till day.
The fells reek of her hearth's scent,
her girdle is greased with lard;
hunger is stayed on her settle, lust in her bed.
Light as spider floss her hair on my cheek which a puff scatters,
light as a moth her fingers on my thigh.
We have eaten and loved and the sun is up,
we have only to sing before parting:
Goodbye, dear love.

Her scones are greased with fat of fried bacon,
her blanket comforts my belly like the south.
We have eaten and loved and the sun is up.
Goodbye.

Applewood, hard to rive,
its knots smoulder all day.
Cobweb hair on the morning,
a puff would blow it away.
Rime is crisp on the bent,
ruts stone-hard, frost spangles fleece.
What breeze will fill that sleeve limp on the line?
A boy's jet steams from the wall, time from the year,
care from deed and undoing.
Shamble, cold, content with beer and pickles,
towards a taciturn lodging amongst strangers.

Where rats go go I,
accustomed to penury,
filth, disgust and fury;
evasive to persist,
reject the bait
yet gnaw the best.
My bony feet
sully shelf and dresser,
keeping a beat in the dark,
rap on lath
till dogs bark
and sleep, shed,
slides from the bed.
O valiant when hunters
with stick and terrier bar escape
or wavy ferret leaps,
encroach and cede again,
rat, roommate, unreconciled.

Stars disperse. We too,
further from neighbours
now the year ages.

V

Drip – icicle's gone.
Slur, ratio, tone,
chime dilute what's done
as a flute clarifies song,
trembling phrase fading to pause
then glow. Solstice past,
years end crescendo.

Winter wrings pigment
from petal and slough
but thin light lays
white next red on sea-crow wing,
gruff sole cormorant
whose grief turns carnival.
Even a bangle of birds
to bind sleeve to wrist
as west wind waves to east
a just perceptible greeting –
sinews ripple the weave,
threads flex, slew, hues meeting,
parting in whey-blue haze.

Mist sets lace of frost
on rock for the tide to mangle.
Day is wreathed in what summer lost.

Conger skimped at the ebb, lobster,
neither will I take, nor troll
roe of its like for salmon.
Let bass sleep, gentles
brisk, skim-grey,
group a nosegay
jostling on cast flesh,
frisk and compose decay
to side shot with flame,
unresting bluebottle wing. Sing,
strewing the notes on the air
as ripples skip in a shallow. Go
bare, the shore is adorned
with pungent weed loudly
filtering sand and sea.

Silver blades of surf
fall crisp on rustling grit,
shaping the shore as a mason
fondles and shapes his stone.

Shepherds follow the links,
sweet turf studded with thrift;
fell-born men of precise instep
leading demure dogs
from Tweed and Till and Teviotdale,
with hair combed back from the muzzle,
dogs from Redesdale and Coquetdale
taught by Wilson or Telfer.
Their teeth are white as birch,
slow under black fringe
of silent, accurate lips.
The ewes are heavy with lamb.
Snow lies bright on Hedgehope
and tacky mud about Till
where the fells have stepped aside
and the river praises itself,
silence by silence sits
and Then is diffused in Now.

Light lifts from the water.
Frost has put rowan down,
a russet blotch of bracken
tousled about the trunk.
Bleached sky. Cirrus
reflects sun that has left
nothing to badger eyes.

Young flutes, harps touched by a breeze,
drums and horns escort
Aldebaran, low in the clear east,
beckoning boats to the fishing.
Capella floats from the north
with shields hung on his gunwale.
That is no dinghy's lantern
occulted by the swell – Betelgeuse,
calling behind him to Rigel.
Starlight is almost flesh.

Great strings next the post of the harp
clang, the horn has majesty,
flutes flicker in the draft and flare.
Orion strides over Farne.
Seals shuffle and bark,
terns shift on their ledges,
watching Capella steer for the zenith,
and Procyon starts his climb.

Furthest, fairest things, stars, free of our humbug,
each his own, the longer known the more alone,
wrapt in emphatic fire roaring out to a black flue.
Each spark trills on a tone beyond chronological compass,
yet in a sextant's bubble present and firm
places a surveyor's stone or steadies a tiller.
Then is Now. The star you steer by is gone,
its tremulous thread spun in the hurricane
spider floss on my cheek; light from the zenith
spun when the slowworm lay in her lap
fifty years ago.

The sheets are gathered and bound,
the volume indexed and shelved,
dust on its marbled leaves.
Lofty, an empty combe,
silent but for bees.
Finger tips touched and were still
fifty years ago.
Sirius is too young to remember.

Sirius glows in the wind. Sparks on ripples
mark his line, lures for spent fish.

Fifty years a letter unanswered;
a visit postponed for fifty years.

She has been with me fifty years.

Starlight quivers. I had day enough.
For love uninterrupted night.

CODA

A strong song tows
us, long earsick.
Blind, we follow
rain slant, spray flick
to fields we do not know.

Night, float us.
Offshore wind, shout,
ask the sea
what's lost, what's left,
what horn sunk,
what crown adrift.

Where we are who knows
of kings who sup
while day fails? Who,
swinging his axe
to fell kings, guesses
where we go?

1965

NOTES

The Northumbrian tongue travel has not taken from me sometimes sounds strange to men used to the koine or to Americans who may not know how much Northumberland differs from the Saxon south of England. Southrons would maul the music of many lines in *Briggflatts*.

An autobiography, but not a record of fact. The first movement is no more a chronicle than the third. The truth of the poem is of another kind.

No notes are needed. A few may spare diligent readers the pains of research.

Spuggies: little sparrows.

May the flower, as haw is the fruit, of the thorn.

Northumbrians should know Eric *Bloodaxe* but seldom do, because all the school histories are written by or for Southrons. Piece his story together from the Anglo-Saxon Chronicle, the Orkneyinga Saga, and Heimskringla, as you fancy.

We have burns in the east, *becks* in the west, but no brooks or creeks.

Oxter: armpit.

Boiled louse: coccus cacti, the cochineal, a parasite on opuntia.

Hillside fiddlers: Pianforini, for instance, or Manini.

Lindisfarne, the Holy Island, where the tracery of the Codex Lindisfarnensis was elaborated.

Saltings: marshy pastures the sea floods at extraordinary springs.

Hastor: a Cockney hero.

The Laughing Stone stands in Tibet. Those who set eyes on it fall into violent laughter which continues till they die. Tibetans are immune, because they have no humour. So the Persian tale relates.

The male salmon after spawning is called a *kelt*.

Gabbro: a volcanic rock.

Aneurin celebrated in the Cymric language the men slain at Catterick by the sons of *Ida,* conquerors of Northumberland.

Skerry: O, come on, you know that one.

Hoy: toss, hurl.

Skillet: an American frying pan; and *girdle,* an English griddle.

Fipple: the soft wood stop forming with part of the hard wood tube the wind passage of a recorder.

Scone: rhyme it with 'on', not, for heaven's sake, 'own'.

Gentles: maggots.

Wilson was less known than *Telfer,* but not less skilful.

Sailors pronounce *Betelgeuse* 'Beetle juice' and so do I. His companion is 'Ridgel', not 'Rhy-ghel'.

Sirius is too young to remember because the light we call by his name left its star only eight years ago; but the light from *Capella,* now in the zenith, set out 45 years ago – as near fifty as makes no difference to a poet.

I have left these notes as they were, with hardly an exception. Notes are a confession of failure, not a palliation of it, still less a reproach to the reader, but may allay some small irritations.
   [BB, Collected Poems]

*   *   *

APPENDICES

Caricature of Basil Bunting published in Italy in 1931.

BASIL BUNTING
A Note on *Briggflatts* (1989)

Briggflatts is a poem: it needs no explanation. The sound of the words spoken aloud is itself the meaning, just as the sound of the notes played on the proper instruments is the meaning of any piece of music. Yet I have been teased so much by people who cannot be content to listen without reasoning, and by people who think they detect in the poem notions alien to it and sometimes repulsive to me that I will set down, if I can, some hint of the state of its maker's mind.

Commonplaces provide the poem's structure: spring, summer, autumn, winter of the year and of man's life, interrupted in the middle and balanced around Alexander's trip to the limits of the world and its futility, and sealed and signed at the end by a confession of our ignorance. Love and betrayal are spring's adventures, the wisdom of elders and the remoteness of death, hardly more than a gravestone. In summer there is no rest from ambition and lust of experience, never final. Those fail who try to force their destiny, like Eric; but those who are resolute to submit, like my version of Pasiphae, may bring something new to birth, be it only a monster.

What Alexander learns when he has thrust his way through the degraded world is that man is contemptibly nothing and yet may live content in humility. Autumn is for reflexion, to set Aneurin's grim elegy against the legend of Cuthbert who saw God in everything, to love without expectation, wander without an inn, persist without hope. Old age can see at last the loveliness of things overlooked or despised, frost, the dancing maggots, sheepdogs, and particularly the stars which make time a paradox and a joke till we can give up our own time, even though we wasted it. And still we know neither where we are nor why.

All old wives' chatter, cottage wisdom. No poem is profound.

The name 'Briggflatts', that of a remote hamlet and a Quaker meeting house, ought to warn people not to look for philosophy. Unfortunately T.S. Eliot's *Four Quartets* are also named after little hidden places, and they do expound the mystical Christianity that nineteenth century theologians brewed from a mash squeezed ultimately, I think, from Plotinus. No scheme of things could be further from my own.

Yeats too professed Plotinus, though his spirit seems nearer to that of Iamblichus. Pound took his gods from Ovid, close cousins to the gods of *The Golden Bough*, never truly pagan but spangles on a

40

neo-Platonic chiffon. Both Pound and Yeats fancied the dreary notion of a history that repeats itself, not as the Buddhists see it, nor as Toynbee, but the cruder Spengler, and that too is part of the neo-Platonic outlook. Pound had too much sense to be consistent. A kind of pragmatism often hidden under the robes of his own private Confucius represents him best. He was not averse to reason, much more a moralist than a metaphysician; yet the scheme of *The Cantos* rests in the mood of Spengler, even, but not consciously, in the mood of Hegel.

Hierarchy and order, the virtues of the neo-Platonic quasi-religion, were prime virtues also to Yeats, Pound and Eliot. They are not virtues to me, only expedients that chafe almost as vilely as the crimes they try to restrain. Amongst philosophers I have most sympathy with Lucretius and his masters, content to explain the world an atom at a time; with Spinoza who saw all things as God, though not with his wish to demonstrate that logically; and with David Hume, the doubter. The men I learned poetry from did not much value these. Perhaps that is why it took me so long to make a poem that reflects, fragmentarily, my whole mind.

Call it God, call it the universe, all we know of it, extended far beyond our telescopes or even inferences, detailed more minutely than our physicists can grope, is less than the histology of a single cell might be to a man's body, or to his conduct. The day's incidents hide our ignorance from us; yet we know it, beneath our routine. In silence, having swept dust and litter from our minds, we can detect the pulse of God's blood in our veins, more persuasive than words, more demonstrative than a diagram. That is what a Quaker meeting tries to be, and that is why my poem is called *Briggflatts*.

Let the incidents and images take care of themselves.

*

This short note on *Briggflatts* constitutes Bunting's only written statement on the poem. His reluctance to publish or circulate such a note in his lifetime is explained in the first two sentences – yet he evidently returned to, and reworked, the piece on various occasions, and intended it to survive him. His intentions in writing the piece are explained also: it only needs to be added that these reasons are as valid now as when they were written. It is in hope of serving a new generation of *Briggflatts* readers that this note is now published. The note exists as a single, untitled, typescript, with autograph alterations, in the Basil Bunting Poetry Archive of Durham University Library, where it is part of the Mountjoy Collection, bought for the Archive by English Estates North. I have made two minor corrections to the text as typed. [...] In other respects the text presented here is Bunting's final text. [RC]

BASIL BUNTING
The Poet's Point of View (1966)

Poetry, like music, is to be heard. It deals in sound – long sounds and short sounds, heavy beats and light beats, the tone relations of vowels, the relations of consonants to one another which are like instrumental colour in music. Poetry lies dead on the page, until some voice brings it to life, just as music, on the stave, is no more than instructions to the player. A skilled musician can imagine the sound, more or less, and a skilled reader can try to hear, mentally, what his eyes see in print: but nothing will satisfy either of them till his ears hear it as real sound in the air. Poetry must be read aloud.

Reading in silence is the source of half the misconceptions that have caused the public to distrust poetry. Without the sound, the reader looks at the lines as he looks at prose, seeking a meaning. Prose exists to convey meaning, and no meaning such as prose conveys can be expressed as well in poetry. That is not poetry's business.

Poetry is seeking to make not meaning, but beauty; or if you insist on misusing words, its "meaning" is of another kind, and lies in the relation to one another of lines and patterns of sound, perhaps harmonious, perhaps contrasting and clashing, which the hearer feels rather than understands, lines of sound drawn in the air which stir deep emotions which have not even a name in prose. This needs no explaining to an audience which gets its poetry by ear. It has neither time nor inclination to seek a prose meaning in poetry.

Very few artists have clear, analytical minds. They do what they do because they must. Some think about it afterwards in a muddled way and try unskilfully to reason about their art. Thus theories are produced which mislead critics and tyros, and sometimes disfigure the work of artists who try to carry out their own theories.

There is no need of any theory for what gives pleasure through the ear, music or poetry. The theoreticians will follow the artist and fail to explain him. The sound, whether it be in words or notes, is all that matters. It is perfectly possible to delight an audience by reading poetry of sufficient quality in a language it does not know. I have seen some of Goethe, some of Hafez, produce nearly the same effect they would have produced on an audience familiar with German or Persian.

Composers are not always the best players of their own compositions, nor poets the best readers of their own verses, though the composer and the poet can always bring out something that might otherwise be lost. Some lack a voice, or have not learned to control it. Some are so immersed in the mechanics of their craft that they, for instance, make an exaggerated pause at the line's end and lose the swing of the metre. Some have mannerisms, such as the constant repetition of a particular cadence, producing an effect rather like the detestable noise parsons make in church. Such defects no doubt sicken some people of poetry readings.

Actors, on the other hand, have the defects of their profession. They cannot bear to leave their beautiful voices in the dark, they must use the whole range on poems that need only a short scale. They are trained for the stage, to make the most of every contrast, and are apt to make poetry sound theatrical. Nevertheless, actors and poets alike, if they but speak the lines, will give you more of a poem than you can get by reading it in silence.

Do not let the people who set examinations kid you that you are any nearer understanding a poem when you have parsed and analysed every sentence, scanned every line, looked up the words in the Oxford Dictionary and the allusions in a library of reference books. That sort of knowledge will make it harder for you to understand the poem because, when you listen to it, you will be distracted by a multitude of irrelevant scraps of knowledge. You will not hear the meaning, which is in the sound.

All the arts are plagued by charlatans seeking money, or fame, or just an excuse to idle. The less the public understands the art, the easier it is for charlatans to flourish. Since poetry reading became popular, they have found a new field, and it is not easy for the outsider to distinguish the fraud from the poet. But it is a little less difficult when poetry is read aloud. Claptrap soon bores. Threadbare work soon sounds thin and broken backed.

There were mountebanks at the famous Albert Hall meeting, as well as a poet or two, but the worst, most insidious charlatans fill chairs and fellowships at universities, write for the weeklies or work for the BBC or the British Council or some other asylum for obsequious idlers. In the eighteenth century it was the Church. If these men had to read aloud in public, their empty lines, without resonance, would soon give them away.

Basil Bunting: 'The Poet's Point of View', *Arts Diary*, Northern Arts (April/ Summer 1966)

BASIL BUNTING
Three other comments

I've never said that poetry consists *only* of sound. I said again and again that the *essential* thing is the sound. Without the sound, there isn't any poetry. But having established it and kept it clear that the sound is the essential, the main thing, you can add all sorts of stuff if you want to. You can, if you like, have as elaborate a system of meanings, sub-meanings, and so forth, as Dante had in the *Divina Commedia*.

FROM Eric Mottram, 'Conversations with Basil Bunting on the occasion of his 75th birthday', broadcast in part on BBC Radio 3, 7 March 1975.

I believe that the fundamental thing in poetry is the sound, so that, whatever the meaning may be, whatever your ultimate intention in that direct might be, if you haven't got the sound right, it isn't a poem. And if you have got it right, it'll get across, even to people who don't understand it. I find it generally works all right if I do read *Briggflatts* with no explanation. The majority of those who hear it, enjoy it, and are moved by it. They certainly do not understand it in a way in which they could go back and write a synopsis of it.

FROM Jonathan Williams & Tom Mayer, 'A Conversation with Basil Bunting', St Andrews Presbyterian College, USA. Both these interviews appeared in *Poetry Information*, 19 (Autumn 1978).

These verses were written here and there now and then over forty years and four continents. Heaped together they make a book.

If ever I learned the trick of it, it was mostly from poets long dead whose names are obvious: Wordsworth and Dante, Horace, Wyat and Malherbe, Manuchehri and Ferdosi, Villon, Whitman, Edmund Spenser; but two living men also taught me much: Ezra Pound and in his sterner, stonier way, Louis Zukofsky. It would not be fitting to collect my poems without mentioning them.

With sleights learned from others and an ear open to melodic analogies I have set down words as a musician pricks his score, not to be read in silence, but to trace in the air a pattern of sound that may sometimes, I hope, be pleasing.

FROM Basil Bunting, Preface to *Collected Poems* (1968).

from **Introduction to *Complete Poems*** (2000)

Basil Bunting's poems should need little or no introduction these days: they have established their individual place amongst the 20th century's finest poetry in English and sound as clearly now as they have ever done – to the delight of the 'unabashed boys and girls' for whom they were composed. Bunting himself kept explication of his poems to an absolute minimum, and I have no intention of departing from that principle – 'Never explain – ' he advised fledgling poets, 'your reader is as smart as you.' A wealth of explanation, biographical and poetical, can be found in the books listed in the bibliography below. Yet some context may help, perhaps, to present this "Centenary Edition" to readers in a new century and to a generation coming to the work without having known the man. I'm happy to accept the invitation of the publishers and the poet's estate to provide such context, whilst encouraging pure poetry-lovers to cut direct to the poems.

Read these poems aloud: Bunting's central statement on poetry, as significant today as it was when first published in 1966, is that 'poetry, like music, is to be heard'. As a statement, this has been picked over, carped at, qualified and explained away by critics ever since, so that it's worth restating it here, in its original, radical essence:

> Poetry, like music, is to be heard. It deals in sound – long sounds and short sounds, heavy beats and light beats, the tone relations of vowels, the relations of consonants to one another... Reading in silence is the source of half the misconceptions that have caused the public to distrust poetry.

Such a conviction was deeply rooted in his upbringing and development, and was the product of a lifetime's practical experience. Born in Scotswood-on-Tyne on 1 March 1900, Bunting grew up close to the vibrant oral traditions of the North-East of England at the start of the 20th century – active traditions of spoken poetry and sung ballads. One of his earliest memories was of his nurse singing Northumbrian folksongs. Such origins remained close to him throughout his eventful life and informed his approach to poetry as much as did his association with modernist contemporaries such as Pound, Eliot and Zukofsky. These undoubted giants of modernism all made nods in their own ways towards the importance of music and sound in their work, but it is left to Bunting, sometime musician, singer and professional music critic, to enunciate the primacy of sound in poetry so extremely, and to put it into practice. Poetry readings were not common when Bunting was undergoing his poetic apprenticeship – nevertheless, he recalled hearing one of his own early Odes (I:3: 'I am agog for foam') recited by Yeats, in the slow, orotund manner of the latter's public readings. Recorded evidence of Bunting's readings is all from the later stages of his life – yet it seems that, from the first, Bunting struck out and away from this grand manner, towards a precise and measured speech which related to that of his Quaker schooling, rather than to the Celtic mists. A full study of the evolution of reading styles of modernism remains to be attempted – nevertheless, we can suggest that Bunting's reading styles (they vary, radically, over time and place) show a marked departure from those of his peers. For today's listener, they retain their vigour and strength over the years and have led through to the most exciting modes of performance which are around today.

We are not all trained readers of poetry today. For the new reader, the first experience of sounding these poems in the air, however inexpertly, will be *physical* – nervous perhaps – but above all enriching. Word patterns which may at first appear dense and complicated on the page become articulated and clarified, resonating across the poems' structure. The subtleties and echoes of language which hold a poem together are revealed by the process of sounding it. Bunting would say that you should hear the "meaning" of the poetry purely in the sound. Some may choose to demur at such an extreme idea – nevertheless, those who have tried it assert that sounding these poems aloud reveals levels of meaning which are lost in silent reading. It's a technique – and a test – which is worth trying on other types of poetry too.

Reading through these poems you may also hear in passing the patient stages in which Bunting's work took shape. First comes the early, self-consciously modernist phase in which he paid his debts to Pound. Next, the increasingly confident and complex period before and immediately after the war when he had found his unique voice and experimented with sound strategies from poetries of many different languages and cultures. Then comes the mature flowering – the "*Briggflatts* period" – following his return to the North-East in the early 1950s. *Briggflatts* itself, Bunting's celebration of northern homeplace and love, was the poem which established his reputation at last, and for many it remains the primary achievement of post-war English poetry. And then finally, towards the very end of the collection you can detect clearly the beginnings of a new phase – denser and more closely structured – which was curtailed by age and death.

Academics will tease out the precise delineations of such zones – 'Follow the clue patiently and you will understand nothing' says Bunting – the point here is to register the ways in which Bunting was always developing and progressing his craft, with a seriousness which can be tracked through his career (Odes I:11, I:36, I:37 and II:6 tell the story). It is this spirit of consistent innovation and discovery, combined with his approach to sound, which has led to Bunting's high status amongst many younger poets today. It has been asserted that there are no direct "heirs" to the poetic tradition of Bunting and other British modernists – and in terms of poets who have slavishly copied his mode of writing that is of course true. Nevertheless, when you read these pages, you will make discoveries which have inspired a great number of emerging British and American poets over the last few decades, and led to developments which are clearly foreshadowed in Bunting's work. 'You are proceeding along the right lines,' wrote Bunting to one apprentice poet, 'They'll lead you beyond the station I stop at, if you keep your mind alive.' If this work was stopped at a station in the late 20th century, it will resonate, we feel, to lively poetic minds long into the 21st.

Bunting's poems accumulated slowly. A youthful slim pamphlet was privately printed in Milan in 1930. Titled *Redimiculum Matellarum* (roughly, 'A Necklace of Chamberpots'), it had one review – from his friend Louis Zukofsky – and otherwise disappeared without trace. His first substantial collection came when he was 50, with the publication of *Poems: 1950* (Cleaner's Press, Galveston, Texas). Here we find for the first time the basic arrangement (Sonatas: Odes: Overdrafts), and to a great extent the sequence of poems which was to be worked on and added to over the next 35 years. *Loquitur* (1965), published in London by Stuart Montgomery's Fulcrum Press, extended the range and tinkered the sequence towards its final form. At the same time came *The Spoils* (from the Morden Tower Bookroom, Newcastle upon Tyne, 1965), and at last, *Briggflatts* (Fulcrum, 1966). The history of the writing of *Briggflatts* – how it was stimulated to a great extent by the crucial encouragement of the young Tyneside poet Tom Pickard, and how, an object lesson in precision, it was cut to its present length from over 2000 lines – is well chronicled elsewhere. *Briggflatts* was a success from the moment it was first performed, appropriately, at Tom and Connie Pickard's Morden Tower in Newcastle, on 22nd December 1965.

Basil Bunting: *Complete Poems*, ed. Richard Caddel (Bloodaxe Books, 2000).

Basil Bunting with his sister Joyce and their cousin Nancy Robson, with the maids Anne and Polly. This photograph was probably taken at the back of the house at 27 Denton Road, Scotswood, c. 1905.

NEIL ASTLEY
Nothing else worth speaking about

'My autobiography is *Briggflatts* – there's nothing else worth speaking about' – BASIL BUNTING (writing to Jonathan Williams)

Basil Bunting was born on 1 March 1900 in Scotswood, Newcastle upon Tyne. His father, Thomas Lowe Bunting, originally from Derbyshire, was the pit doctor for Montague Colliery as well as a Newcastle GP. His mother Annie, *née* Cheesman, came from Throckley, where her father was the colliery manager. His sister Joyce was born two years later.

Basil Bunting spent his childhood in Newcastle – the early years at 27 Denton Road, Scotswood – but his strongest sense of locality and culture came from the Cheesmans and their circle in Throckley, Northumberland – where he later lived between long periods spent abroad. The family speech – like his own – was strongly Northumbrian in character, marked in particular by the Throckley dialect with its soft burr and rolling 'r's. His mother was related to several Border families, including the Charltons, and as a child he delighted in stories and songs of the Border reivers. He wanted to write poetry from an early age, describing this later to Jonathan Williams as 'a genuine childhood desire, an instinct' – encouraged by his father's reading of 'the less recondite Wordsworth' and other poets to the family. His father and aunt helped foster his deep appreciation of music.

His early education was at a Dame's school run by Miss A.M. Bell at West Parade, Rye Hill. At the age of 12, he began a Quaker schooling away from home, boarding first at Ackworth School, Yorkshire (1912-16) and then at Leighton Park in Berkshire (1916-18). The Bunting family meanwhile moved house to Fenham, then a leafier middle-class Newcastle suburb; later they moved to Jesmond, where they remained until the death of his father in 1925.

While at Leighton Park he came across an early edition of Whitman's *Leaves of Grass* in the school library. Enthusiastic about its musical cadences – which he likened to what Liszt was doing in music – he wrote an appreciation of the work which won a national essay prize, attracting the attention of Edward Carpenter, one of Whitman's closest friends, who cycled from Sheffield to call upon the 15-year-old critic.

ABOVE: *Basil Bunting (on the right), c. 1913.*

OPPOSITE: *Peggy pictured in front of the Greenbanks' house at Brigflatts.*

In 1913 he spent the first of many holidays at the small Cumbrian Quaker hamlet of Brigflatts with the family of his school friend John Greenbank, whose sister Peggy was the adolescent sweetheart remembered in *Briggflatts* (which is dedicated to her), and began attending meetings at the 17th-century meeting house. His formative visits to Brigflatts in his teens were enormously important to him, both in terms of personal experience and his later remembrance and embodiment of that time in his poetry.

(It should be noted that Brigflatts the place has one *g*, but Bunting spells it *Briggflatts*. Also, while Brigflatts was then in Cumberland – east of the Eden valley, and now part of Cumbria – Bunting was not alone in viewing that part of the northern Pennines as Northumbrian.)

Writing in later life to Louis Zukofsky (16 December 1964), Bunting acknowledged the debt he felt he owed to

> Peggy Greenbank, and her whole ambience, the Rawthey valley, the fells of Lunedale, the Viking inheritance all spent save the faint smell of it, the ancient Quaker life accepted without thought and without suspicion that it might seem eccentric: and what happens when one deliberately thrusts love aside, as I then did – it has its revenge. That must be a longish poem.

Basil Bunting: studio portrait, 1917.

Portrait of the artist as a young man.

In his excellent study, *Bunting: The Shaping of His Verse*, Peter Makin tells how George Fox came to Brigflatts in 1652, and how his vision of 'a great people in white raiment by the river's side' came to pass when groups of Seekers gathered by the River Rawthey after his visit. Fox's message to them the following Sunday is said to be the founding event of Quakerism.

Profoundly affected by his Quaker education, Bunting stopped short of becoming a member of the Society of Friends. As a pacifist, he refused to fight in the First World War, and this 'conchy's appeal' was widely reported in the local press:

> A conscientious objector to military service, who had reached in March last the mature age of 18 years, came before the Newcastle Tribunal yesterday. In a long statement the lad, who carried himself with great self-possession, objected to war, to noncombatant service because it released a man for combatancy, to national service because it helped the prosecution of war...
> [*North Mail*, 18 April 1918]

> [*'Newcastle "Conchy" Would sooner see Huns Over-running Country Than Kill a Man'*...] He had been educated at a Quaker school, where the whole atmosphere was one of pacifism.
> [*Illustrated Chronicle*, 18 April 1918]

The 18-year-old Bunting was imprisoned, first at the notorious Newcastle Guardroom at Fenham Barracks, and later at Wormwood Scrubs. After a long spell in a military hospital on Salisbury Plain being treated for a septic ulcer, he was sent to do hard labour in Winchester Prison, remaining there long after the Armistice, until May 1919, when he absconded to London while on sick leave following a hunger strike. The prison regime was harsh, with rough treatment and scant rations. Bunting was reticent about his time in prison, but his depiction of the imprisoned poet's state of mind and sensory deprivation in *Villon* – written six years later – is clearly marked by traumatic experiences.

After a short period of study at the London School of Economics, this conscientious objector became secretary in 1922 to Harry Barnes, MP for East Newcastle, who had been Commanding Officer of the 2nd Volunteer Battalion Northumberland Fusiliers in the War. But he found the work dull and soon began a life of wandering and penury.

Throughout this time Bunting was continually trying to write poetry as close to music as possible – and working very much on his own – but every advance required the destruction of all previous efforts. The earliest surviving Bunting poem is a small fragment dating from 1923.

This picture of Basil Bunting with his cousin Basil Cheesman and Jack the dog was taken in Northumberland after his release from prison, c. 1920.

ABOVE: *Basil Bunting, 1923.* BELOW LEFT: *Ezra Pound.* RIGHT: *Louis Zukofsky.*

He first encountered the work of Ezra Pound and T.S. Eliot in 1919. In her study, Barbara E. Lesch quotes his comment that although he had felt the resemblance of Eliot's *Preludes* to Chopin's was 'slight and superficial', he was 'delighted to discover that there were actually people doing what I had merely worked out in my head was the kind of thing that ought to be done. This was a revelation that it really could be done, that it wasn't a hopeless trade.'

In 1923 he was living in Paris, working as a road-digger, artists' model and barman, when he met Pound 'playing a swashbuckling kind of chess'. Writing later to a friend, in 1932, he described the encounter:

> I believed then as now, that is *Propertius* was the finest of modern poems. Indeed, it was the one that gave me the notion that poetry wasn't altogether impossible in the XX century. So I made friends. I was digging roads outside of Paris for a living. I got locked up for a colossal drunk. It was Ezra who discovered me…and perjured himself in the courts to try to get me off. When I came out of quod, and was working at the Jocky, he introduced me to Ford Madox Ford and I became sub. ed. and sec. to the *Transatlantic Review*.

In 1924 he followed Pound to Rapallo in Italy, giving up his job to Ernest Hemingway (whom he later berated for his 'unlaughable caricature' of Ford in *A Moveable Feast*, 'a lie…deliberately assembled to damage the reputation of a dead man'). He wrote his first major poem, *Villon*, in 1925, which was much admired by Eliot as well as by Pound, but for the next 40 years his work was only published by poetry magazines and small presses, receiving no wider public acknowledgement.

Returning to England shortly before his father's death in 1925, he lived for the next two years with his mother in Throckley (at 242 Newburn Road, known locally as The Villas), teaching miners and unemployed workmen at the Lemington Adult School. For the next 30 years he would return to The Villas whenever he was unable to make a living elsewhere.

By 1928 he was working as a reviewer or music critic for London weeklies, but living in a cottage at Coldside Farm in the Simonsides, where he absorbed many aspects of rural Northumberland life (including the training of sheep dogs) he later drew upon in his poetry, supported in part by a gift of £200 per year from a wealthy American patron, Margaret de Silver

In 1929 he returned to his wanderings, first to Berlin and then back to Rapallo, where he was known to W.B. Yeats as 'one of Pound's

Photograph of Rapallo taken by Bunting with his boat in the foreground.

more savage disciples'. And in 1929, in Venice, he met a young American graduate, Marian Gray Culver, from Eau Claire, Wisconsin, who was touring Europe. Looking down from her hotel balcony at a Venetian festival, she saw Bunting, who began explaining the celebration to her. Three days later, they moved in together, and were married on Long Island in 1930, the year when his first slim volume of poems was published in Milan under the title *Redimiculum Matellarum* (which means 'a necklace of chamber-pots').

They lived in New York for much of that Depression year, with Bunting trying unsuccessfully to find work using letters of introduction from Pound. However, he was able to see more of Louis Zukofsky, whom he had first met in Rapallo, and their lifelong friendship dates from this time. Marian also introduced him to other friends, including René Taupin, William Carlos Williams, Adolf Dehn and Tibor Serly. But eventually Pound persuaded him that he might as well be unemployed in Rapallo as in New York, as Bunting later told Jonathan Williams:

> It was better to go back and see how long we could live on nothing in Italy – rather than the very short time you can live on nothing in the United States. [...] We settled down at Rapallo half-way up the mountain, and on the whole it was a very pleasant time. I got a good deal of poetry written. I enjoyed conversation, enjoyed sailing my boat, enjoyed the sunshine. And enjoyed having a baby. My first daughter. Pound was there and various other people. Yeats was there. I saw a good deal of Yeats. But of few others.

Five years after its completion, *Villon* was finally published, in the October 1930 issue of *Poetry*, and Bunting's output during this productive period in Rapallo included *Chomei at Toyama*, *Attis*, *Aus dem zweiten Reich* and a number of shorter poems. Their daughter Bourtai was born in Genoa in 1931, and her sister Roudaba in 1934, by which time they were living in the Canaries, with Bunting trying to write poetry and journalism, still struggling to support his family with some help from Margaret de Silver. On one occasion – which must have been in 1936 – Bunting is said to have played chess with General Franco, then General Commandant of the Canaries.

One high point during this financially depressing time was the first major appearance of Bunting's poetry in an important British publication. Ezra Pound's *Active Anthology*, dedicated to Bunting and Zukofsky, 'two strugglers in the desert', published by Faber in October 1933, contained a large selection of Bunting's work.

ABOVE: *Self portait in mirror, 1929.*

OPPOSITE ABOVE: *Bunting on the beach with Marian at Rapallo, 1933.*

OPPOSITE BELOW: *Marian, Bunting and Helen Lehmann, Rapallo, 1933.*

Passport photograph, 1930s.

Bunting in Barcelona, 1933.

Santa Cruz, 1934: Minoletti, Masoliver, Bunting, Haas.

*The Bunting children: Rustam, Roudaba, Bourtai in America in 1939
(photographed through gauze as a silhouette profile picture).*

ABOVE: *Squadron-Leader Bunting with colleagues in Persia, 1945.*

BELOW: *Bunting reading: picture taken in Persia.*

Although Pound remained – with Louis Zukofsky – his main literary influence – Bunting began to distance himself from him 'as Pound's political views became increasingly maniacally fascist' (Caddel & Flowers).

After two years on Tenerife, shortly before the outbreak of the Spanish Civil War, the Buntings left for England, and spent the next year in London. In 1937 they separated, with Marian taking their two daughters to America, where their son Rustam was born (he died from polio at 16, never having met his father); three years later she was granted a divorce in Wisconsin. Bunting meanwhile bought a boat called the *Thistle* for £100, and for the next year sailed around the coasts of Essex and Devon, working with the herring fishermen.

In 1938 he enrolled at Nellist's Nautical School in Summerhill Terrace, Newcastle, not for marine certification, which his bad eyesight prevented, but just 'to know enough to handle a boat intelligently'. This peculiar cramming school for mates or masters was run by two eccentric brothers with no seafaring qualifications, but nevertheless was credited at the time with turning out nearly half the Merchant Navy Officers in Britain.

For the next year Bunting skippered a millionaire's schooner, visiting Canada and the USA, returning to England in 1939, wanting to serve in the impending conflict – he saw war as necessary this time if Hitler was to be stopped. Unable to find work initially – except to give WEA lectures on history in Morpeth – he could not get into a service unit because of his poor eyesight, until a sympathetic doctor friend of his late father allowed him to learn the eye-test by heart, by which means he was able to enter the RAF.

After spending the first years of the War in balloon operations, and then as an aircraftsman in Iraq, he became an intelligence officer, and by 1945 had become Squadron-Leader Bunting and Vice-Consul of Isfahan in Persia, where he had initially been posted as an interpreter, because of his knowledge of Persian, albeit the medieval variety (which he had learned in order to read the classical Persian poets). But as he later recalled: 'I never expected to hear a word of it spoken until I arrived in Persia and was called upon to interpret for a court martial. You can imagine how difficult that was. I hope they put the right man in jail. Very fortunately it wasn't one of those cases where it would require shooting or hanging.' His later war service included taking a convoy of shells across the North African desert, a month-long nightmare he later drew upon in *The Spoils*.

After the War, he served as chief of political intelligence in Tehran, and in 1948 met and married a young Kurdo-Armenian girl, Sima

Photographs taken by Bunting in Persia. Isfahan Majet Shah Mosque, 1947 (top left), with a plaster detail (top right). Mashad, 1948 (below).

Alladallian. Their daughter Maria was born in Persia in 1950. For the next three years he worked for spells as the *Times* correspondent in Tehran, and because of his expert local knowledge was the only foreign correspondent able to file accurate reports from a country in political turmoil, so much so that on one occasion a crowd was incited to seize him. As the fanatics shrieked 'Death to Bunting!' outside the hotel where all the foreign journalists were sheltering, the *Times* correspondent was nowhere to be seen, but when questioned afterwards said he had been amongst the mob waving copies

Bunting with his second wife Sima, Tehran, 1948.

of his paper and yelling 'Death to Bunting!' as vociferously as the next zealot. According to Keith Alldritt's colourful biography, *The Poet as Spy: The Life and Wild Times of Basil Bunting*, Bunting was still working then for British Intelligence

Expelled in 1952 by the new Iranian leader Mossadeq, Bunting drove his family to England in a dilapidated car, a journey which took a month. They moved back in with his mother at Throckley, where their son Thomas was born. By then in his 50s – with no formal qualifications – Bunting was unable to find a job for some time, apart from some poorly paid part-time work for the *Manchester Guardian* and proof-reading for the Coal Board's journal *Mining*.

During this time he was deeply affected by the continued neglect of his poetry. While he had been living in Persia, his first full-length book, *Poems 1950*, had been published by a small press in Texas, but this sank without trace. Although his long poem *The Spoils* then

Morden Tower, Newcastle: The Tower has changed little since this picture was taken in 1899. Built around 1280, it stands on the longest remaining stretch of Newcastle's city walls. In 1620, the Company of Plumbers, Plasterers and Glaziers, who had occupied the Tower since 1536, added another storey to the building. This is the room at the top of the steps where poetry readings were first held in 1964. By the 1960s the buildings to the right were small factories, warehouses and a night club; today the Tower is flanked by the back kitchens of Newcastle's Chinatown district.

appeared in the influential American magazine *Poetry* in 1951, his work was still little regarded outside a small circle of admirers – mainly fellow poets – and mostly in America. Attempts to publish his work foundered in Britain. Poetry editors weren't especially interested in modernist poetry, except for T.S. Eliot at Faber, who declined to publish what would have been the first British edition of Bunting's poems in May 1951.

In 1954, Bunting finally secured regular employment as a sub-editor on the *Newcastle Daily Journal*, working the evening shift from 5 P.M. to 2 A.M. six days a week, and using a moped for transport. In 1957 he moved with his mother and family to Wylam, and was able to transfer to the day shift of the sister paper, the *Evening Chronicle*, for which he worked until retiring in 1966. The daily grind of subbing financial pages and shipping lists was stultifying, but he used this period to keep writing, filling notebooks on the daily train ride between Wylam and Newcastle. Also working on the *Evening Chronicle* during the latter period was Barry MacSweeney, who had left school at 16 to become a cub reporter on the paper.

The cultural revolution of the 1960s saw poetry revivals centred in Newcastle, Liverpool and London. Its focus in Newcastle was the Morden Tower turret room on the city's medieval walls, where Tom and Connie Pickard started putting on poetry readings in June 1964. Pickard had written for advice to Jonathan Williams at Jargon Press in North Carolina, who suggested he get in touch with Basil Bunting, a writer none of Pickard's writer friends in Newcastle had heard of, let alone read:

> One Sunday night shortly after receiving Jonathan's letter, I decided to look up Mr Bunting in the telephone directory, and I gave him a ring from a public box. […] Nervously I explained I was putting together a magazine and wanted some contributions from him. He invited me over and I caught the next train out.

After reading him *The Spoils*, Bunting 'approved our plans to open Morden Tower and offered what help he could give'.

His meeting with Pickard was the catalyst which transformed Bunting's life and reputation. As well as giving him a highly receptive young audience of poetry enthusiasts, Morden Tower republished *The Spoils*, and many famous poets of the time came to Newcastle, not just to read at the Tower but to meet and talk to Bunting, from Allen Ginsberg and Robert Creeley to Hugh MacDiarmid and Lawrence Ferlinghetti. Stimulated by this contact with poets and poetry readers, and most importantly by his continuing correspondence with Zukofsky,

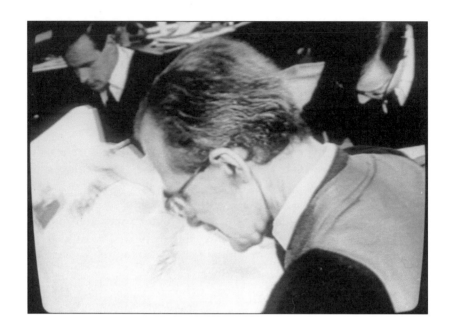

Two stills from a BBC Television documentary made in 1966. ABOVE, *Bunting working on the* Evening Chronicle; BELOW, *pictured on his nightly journey home on the train to Wylam, supposedly still writing* Briggflatts *in his notebook.*

OPPOSITE: *Bunting pictured when he was working on the* Evening Chronicle *in Newcastle, in 1965, before the eye operation which greatly improved his sight.*

Bunting toiled over the next year on his master work, *Briggflatts*, buoyed up by Tom Pickard's enthusiasm and – as the myth has it – wanting to show the young poet how to write a long poem.

Bunting called *Briggflatts* his 'autobiography'. It is a complex work, drawing on many elements of his life, experience and knowledge. Cut from an alleged 2000 lines to around 700, its structural models include Scarlatti sonatas and the latticework of the Lindisfarne Gospels. After the first public reading of the poem at Morden Tower on 22 December 1965, *Briggflatts* was published in 1966 in Chicago in *Poetry* and then in London by Fulcrum Press, an imprint renowned in the 60s for contemporary, experimental poetry.

Briggflatts was immediately hailed as a major work, with Cyril Connolly calling it 'the finest long poem to have been published in England since T.S. Eliot's *Four Quartets*'. In 1966 Bunting was able to resign from his newspaper job to take up a visiting lectureship at the University of California, Santa Barbara. In Wisconsin he met his daughters Bourtai and Roudaba again for the first time in 30 years, and from then on was always in touch with his American family. Another highlight that summer was meeting Lorine Niedecker, whose work he had greatly admired for many years.

In 1968 Bunting was given a two-year appointment as Northern Arts Literary Fellow at the Universities of Durham and Newcastle, and his first *Collected Poems* was published by Fulcrum. Hugh Mac-Diarmid wrote that Bunting's poems 'are the most important which have appeared in any form of the English language since T.S. Eliot's *The Waste Land*'.

In 1977, the Buntings separated, and for four years the ageing poet had to live in a tiny box-like house in Washington New Town, far from his beloved Northumberland fells. In 1981, however, he was able to move into a cottage at Greystead, Tarset, in the North Tyne Valley, where he lived for three years until he had to move again in 1984, this time to Fox Cottage at Whitley Chapel in Hexhamshire.

Basil Bunting died after a short illness on 17 April 1985 in Hexham General Hospital. A stone bearing his name and dates marks the place where his ashes were strewn in the burial ground at Briggflats.

For some years Bunting's work was published by Oxford University Press. Following the much criticised closure of the OUP poetry list, Bloodaxe Books published its centenary edition of the *Complete Poems* with a double-cassette of audio recordings in 2000.

This biographical sketch is indebted especially to two previous publications, *Basil Bunting: A Northern Life* by Richard Caddel and Anthony Flowers (Newcastle Libraries, 1997) and *The Poetry of Basil Bunting* by Victoria Forde (Bloodaxe Books, 1991), with additional detail from various sources included in the Selected Bibliography.

Basil Bunting with Ted Hughes at Lumb Bank, Yorkshire, in 1982, when he judged the Arvon Poetry Competition with Michael Baldwin, George Barker, Gwendolyn Brooks, Adrian Mitchell, Peter Redgrove and Stephen Spender.

DON SHARE
Short notes on a longish poem

Basil Bunting had written to Louis Zukofsky as early as 1953 that 'I shall have to try again to write a QED sonata to earn the hatred of all the tasteful critics and a few centuries of misrepresentation but convince all candid listeners and so survive.' In mid–December 1964, Bunting wrote to an old friend, the actor and poet Denis Goacher, about his interest in the form of the long poem, which was 'much neglected'. Working on a draft of one while riding the train to and from his job as a subeditor at the *Newcastle Evening Chronicle*, he claimed to have filled 'two fat notebooks absolutely chocked full, front and back, both sides of the page'. Roy Fisher recalled Bunting telling him in the spring of 1965 that 'the music is complete; all I have to do is to make adjustments to the content' and Gael Turnbull recorded in a journal entry for 15 May receipt of a letter announcing the poem's completion. (Intriguingly, an early poem of Turnbull's published in 1956 was called, 'An Irish Monk on Lindisfarne, about 650 AD' – Bunting owned several volumes by Turnbull.) In June, Bunting sent the finished poem to *Poetry* magazine in Chicago, and on 10 August 1965, Bunting wrote Henry Rago, the editor of *Poetry*:

> I know the difficulties of finding even a modest amount of space in a well-run magazine let alone about 750 lines; and you, no doubt, know the impatience of authors. There is a momentary spate of publicity about me in England at present and I would like to have taken advantage of it to get a good circulation for whoever presently makes a pamphlet of *Briggflatts*, particularly as several publishers seem determined to bring out my collected poems sometime next year, which will limit the time available for selling a pamphlet; but it is more important to me to appear in *Poetry*, which published my Villon 35 years ago and nearly everything considerable I have written since... I had also better say that I know there are inaccurate and incomplete mss copies floating around. It has been more copied by industrious penmen than any poem I ever heard of, Lord knows why, one copying down another's errors and so on. Over that I have no control. I suppose it is theoretically possible that some pirate might print one of these garbled copies without consulting me, but I don't believe it. I'd make one hell of a fuss if it happened. But the existence of this curious mss circulation is another reason for hastening the printing as much as possible.

In an interview, Bunting remarked that he worked from 'one little notebook, two little notebooks, completely full both sides of each page, with the cuttings out and so forth. And I reckon roughly twenty-thousand words, twenty-thousand lines I mean, to get my seven hundred.' The notebook material held by the Poetry/Rare Books Collection at the University of Buffalo, State University of New York, consists of one book as well a number of loose leaves that may or may not be from a second notebook. Bunting wrote first on recto pages, numbering them in the upper right-hand corner, then flipped the book over and wrote on verso pages, left unnumbered. He would try out a number of lines and expand these into sections of verse. Then he would rewrite the sections, incorporating revisions, and in some cases cancel the earlier sections. When a section had been finished, a new one was begun and worked on. At times, he drew scansion marks above or near certain lines. Some of the loose leaves can be interpolated successfully if either page numbers or repeated lines of verse make this possible; others seem orphaned, and may be from a second notebook of the same size. Bunting's handwriting in this material is not always easy to decipher, although in other autograph manuscript material, e.g. fair copies of poems, it is usually quite clear; this may support Bunting's claim that he worked on the notebooks while he was commuting to work. Many cancellations of entire sections consist of single diagonal strokes; horizontal lines are often drawn through individual words or phrases, but when Bunting has scratched out words or phrases they are difficult to reconstruct. The redundancy of material makes it fairly straightforward to correlate it with the published version of the poem. The notebook material also includes a number of drawings and some incidental text, e.g., a letter of recommendation on behalf of Tom Pickard, a mailing address, etc.

Bunting's bibliographer Roger Guedalla claims that 'the poem was written, so Bunting has wryly suggested, to show Tom Pickard how to write a long poem. It was originally 15,000 lines long and was reduced to its final 700 lines over a long period of time. The author prepared about twelve copies which he typed out and sent to various friends. This version is longer than the final published version.' However, Caddel in his edition of the *Collected Poems*, noted that there is no evidence to support the claim of a longer version in typescript. The Olin Library at Washington University, St Louis, holds the carbon copy of the poem in typescript (*ca.* 1965) Bunting sent to Robert Creeley; it is not substantially different from the printed version.

*

On the general composition of *Briggflatts*

Bunting said: 'I use anything as subject. Mostly I've written a poem that is concrete before I've got a subject. I know what shape it's going to be. I sometimes know, even in considerable detail, what the rhythm will be before I've got any notion of what is going to be said in it. *Briggflatts* began as a diagram on a piece of paper. I added a Latin motto to remind me of the kind of mood I wanted. It developed in that sort of way. In fact, the first line of the poem is the last, apart from the coda – it is a matter of filling out the form. [...] My forms are [...] much larger, the architectonics are the poetry really... It's finding the actual building materials to suit the architect's design, not designing the building to suit the materials that happen to be lying around.' Bunting reproduced this diagram during an interview, and explained: 'You have a poem. You're going to have five parts because it's got to be an uneven number. So that the central one should be the one apex, there [pointing to diagram]. But what is new, the only new thing that I knew of in, in doing it, was that instead of having one climax in the other parts you have two. In the first two the climax is the less and another immediately comes out of it when you're not expecting it. So you have it for those two. In the others the first climax is the greater and it trails off. [...] If you add to that the Coda which came accidentally more or less, you've got the diagram of the whole poem.'

'Once I had got the thing clear in my head as a diagram, I simply set to work and wrote it, writing when I could. Three lines in the train on the way to work, three lines on the way home from work. Saturday mornings when there was not much to do, because there's no stock exchange on Saturday morning, I'd get perhaps ten or fifteen lines written – and always the cutting out and the buggering about and the buggering about and the rewriting and so on.' [...]

Late in his life, Bunting commented that a 'very short narrative – nine stanzas – was needed to set the key for *Briggflatts*. For the rest, I'd learned from Spenser that there's no need to tell the reader what he can see for himself.'

Basil Bunting: Selected Bibliography

Most publication on Bunting, significantly, has happened since his death – he would surely never have approved personally of much of it. Nevertheless, the reader looking for more information on his work has now a range of sources in print and online to which to turn, and some – notably the Makin and Forde titles – are excellent. The following, it must be stressed, is a highly selective list. [RC/NA]

Agenda, 16 no. 1 (Spring 1978): Basil Bunting special issue.

Keith Alldritt: *Modernism in the Second World War: the later poetry of Ezra Pound, T.S. Eliot, Basil Bunting, and Hugh MacDiarmid* (New York: Peter Lang, 1989).

Keith Aldritt: *The Poet as Spy: The Life and Wild Times of Basil Bunting* (London: Aurum Press, 1998).

Tony Baker: 'On Basil Bunting', *Jacket*, 12 (July 2000).

Basil Bunting: *Basil Bunting on Poetry*, edited by Peter Makin (Baltimore: Johns Hopkins University Press, 2000).

Basil Bunting: *Basil Bunting reads 'Briggflatts' and other poems* [double-cassette set] (Newcastle upon Tyne: Bloodaxe Books, 2000). Includes *Briggflatts*, *Villon*, *The Spoils*, selected Odes and Overdrafts.

Basil Bunting: *Bunting's Persia*, edited by Don Share (Chicago: Flood Editions, 2011).

Basil Bunting: *Briggflatts*, with Stream Records audio recording (1966) on CD and Peter Bell's film *Basil Bunting: An introduction to the work of a poet* (1982) on DVD (Tarset: Bloodaxe Books, 2009).

Basil Bunting: *Complete Poems*, edited by Richard Caddel (Newcastle upon Tyne: Bloodaxe Books, 2000; New York: New Directions, 2003; Toronto: Penguin Books, Canada, 2003).

Basil Bunting: *The Poems*, scholarly annotated edition edited by Don Share (London: Faber & Faber, 2010).

Basil Bunting: *The Recordings of Basil Bunting* [8 cassette tapes], edited by Richard Swigg (Keele: Keele University in association with the Basil Bunting Poetry Centre, 1994).

Basil Bunting: *Three Essays*, edited by Richard Caddel (Durham: Basil Bunting Poetry Centre, 1994).

Bête Noire, 2/3 (Spring 1987): Basil Bunting special issue.

Gordon Brown (ed.): *High on the Walls: an anthology celebrating twenty-five years of poetry readings at Morden Tower* (Newcastle upon Tyne: Morden Tower/Bloodaxe Books, 1990).

David Burnett: *Basil Bunting* (Durham: Durham University Library, 1987).

Richard Caddel (ed.): *Sharp Study and Long Toil: Basil Bunting Special Issue* (Durham: *Durham University Journal* in association with the Basil Bunting Poetry Centre, 1995).

Richard Caddel & Anthony Flowers: *Basil Bunting: A Northern Life* (Newcastle upon Tyne: Newcastle Libraries and Information Service in association with the Basil Bunting Poetry Centre, 1997).

Garth Clucas: 'Basil Bunting: A Chronology', *Poetry Information*, 19 (Autumn 1978),

Kenneth Cox: 'The Aesthetic of Basil Bunting', *Agenda*, 4 no. 3 (Autumn 1966), 20-28.

Kenneth Cox: 'Basil Bunting', *Scripsi*, 3 nos 2 & 3 (August 1985), 1-5.

Kenneth Cox: 'Basil Bunting reading Wordsworth', *Jacket*, 28 (October 2005).

Kenneth Cox: 'A Commentary on Basil Bunting's *Villon*', *Agenda*, 16 no 1 (Spring 1978), 20-36; *Stony Brook*, nos. 3-4 (1969), 59-69.

Peter Craven & Michael Heyward: 'An Interview with Basil Bunting', *Scripsi*, 1 nos. 3-4 (April 1982), 27-31.

Robert Creeley: 'A Note on Basil Bunting', *Agenda*, 4 no. 3 (Autumn 1966), 18-19.

Donald Davie: 'Privately Published', *New Statesman*, 72 (4 November 1966), 672.

Donald Davie: *Under Briggflatts: A History of Poetry in Great Britain 1960-1988* (Manchester: Carcanet Press, 1989).

Sean Figgis & Andrew McAllister: 'Basil Bunting: The Last Interview', *Bête Noire*, 2/3 (Spring 1987), 22-51.

Victoria Forde: *The Poetry of Basil Bunting* (Newcastle upon Tyne: Bloodaxe Books, 1991).

Georgia Straight Writing Supplement, 6 (18-24 November 1970): Basil Bunting special issue.

Roger Guedalla: *Basil Bunting: A Bibliography of Works and Criticism* (Norwood, PA: Norwood Editions, 1973).

Barbara E. Lesch: *Basil Bunting: A Major British Modernist*, Ph.D. dissertation (University of Wisconsin, 1979).

Hugh Kenner: 'Never a Boast or a See Here', *National Review*, 19 (31 October 1967), 1217-18.

Hugh Kenner: 'A Resurrected Poet', *Poetry*, 78 (September 1951), 19.

Peter Makin: *Bunting: The Shaping of his Verse* (Oxford: Clarendon Press, 1992).

Eric Mottram: 'Conversation with Basil Bunting on the Occasion of his 75th Birthday', *Poetry Information* 19 (Autumn 1978), 3-10.

Paideuma 9 no. 1 (Spring 1980): Basil Bunting special issue.

Jenny Penberthy: 'Brief Words Are Hard to Find: Basil Bunting and Lorine Niedecker', *Conjunctions*, 8 (1985).

Poetry Information 19 (Autumn 1978): Basil Bunting special issue.

Richard Price & James McGonigal: *The Star You Steer By: Basil Bunting and British Modernism* (Amsterdam & Atlanta: Rodopi Editions, 2000).

Herbert Read: 'Basil Bunting: Music or Meaning', *Agenda*, 4 no. 3 (Autumn 1966),. 4-10.

Peter Quartermain: *Basil Bunting: Poet of the North* (Durham: Basil Bunting Poetry Centre, 1990).

Peter Quartermain & Warren Tallman: 'Basil Bunting Talks about *Briggflatts*', *Agenda*, 16, no.1 (Spring 1978), 3-19.

Poetry Information, 19 (Autumn 1978): Basil Bunting special issue.

Dale Reagan: 'An Interview with Basil Bunting', *Montemora*, 3 (Spring 1977), 67-80.

Scripsi, 1 nos. 3-4 (April 1982): Basil Bunting special issue.

Antony Suter: 'Musical Structure in the Poetry of Basil Bunting', *Agenda*, 16, no.1 (1978), 46-54.

Antony Suter: 'Time and the Literary Past in the Poetry of Basil Bunting', *Contemporary Literature*, 12 no. 4 (Autumn 1971), 510-26.

Brian Swann: 'Basil Bunting of Northumberland', *St Andrew's Review*, 4 no. 2 (Spring-Summer 1977), 33-41.

Carroll F. Terrell (ed.): *Basil Bunting: Man and Poet* (Orono, Maine, USA: National Poetry Foundation, 1981).

Charles Tomlinson: 'Experience into Music: The Poetry of Basil Bunting', *Agenda*, 4 no. 3 (Autumn 1966).

Jonathan Williams (ed.): *Descant on Rawthey's Madrigal: Conversations with Basil Bunting* (Lexington, KY: Gnomon Press, 1968).

Jonathan Williams (ed.): *Madeira & toasts for Basil Bunting's 75th birthday* (Dentdale: Jargon Society, 1975).

Jonathan Williams & Tom Meyer: 'A Conversation with Basil Bunting', *Poetry Information* 19 (1978), 37-47.

Christian Wiman: 'Free of our humbug: notes on Basil Bunting', *New Criterion*, 27 no. 8 (April 2004).

R.S. Woof: 'Basil Bunting's Poetry', *Stand*, 8 no. 2 (1966), 28-34.

Letters to Louis Zukofsky, 1930-1964. Harry Ransom Humanities Research Center, University of Texas at Austin. This collection includes many letters from Basil Bunting.